T0266213

THE AUTISTIC ALICE

Joanne Limburg was born in London in 1970, and studied Philosophy at Cambridge. She has since gained an MA in Psychoanalytic Studies, worked as an Associate Lecturer for the Open University, and was the Royal Literary Fund Fellow at Magdalen College, Cambridge, from 2008 to 2010. She won an Eric Gregory Award for her poetry in 1998, and has published three collections with Bloodaxe: *Femenismo* (2000) was shortlisted for the Forward Prize for Best First Collection; *Paraphernalia* (2007) was a Poetry Book Society Recommendation; *The Autistic Alice* (2017) is her third collection.

Her other books include *The Woman Who Thought Too Much* (Atlantic Books, 2010), a memoir about OCD, anxiety and poetry; *Bookside Down: poems for the modern, discerning cyber-kid* (Salt Publishing, 2013), an anthology for younger readers; her novel, *A Want of Kindness: a novel of Queen Anne* (Atlantic Books, 2015); and *Letters to My Weird Sisters: On Autism and Feminism* (Atlantic Books, 2021).

She was made a Fellow of the Royal Society of Literature in 2022.

JOANNE LIMBURG

The Autistic Alice

BLOODAXE BOOKS

Copyright © Joanne Limburg 2017

ISBN: 978 1 78037 343 0

First published 2017 by
Bloodaxe Books Ltd,
Eastburn,
South Park,
Hexham,
Northumberland NE46 1BS.

www.bloodaxebooks.com
For further information about Bloodaxe titles
please visit our website or write to
the above address for a catalogue.

Supported using public funding by
ARTS COUNCIL
ENGLAND

LEGAL NOTICE

All rights reserved. No part of this book may be
reproduced, stored in a retrieval system, or
transmitted in any form, or by any means, electronic,
mechanical, photocopying, recording or otherwise,
without prior written permission from Bloodaxe Books Ltd.

Requests to publish work from this book
must be sent to Bloodaxe Books Ltd.

Joanne Limburg has asserted her right under
Section 77 of the Copyright, Designs and Patents Act 1988
to be identified as the author of this work.

Cover design: Neil Astley & Pamela Robertson-Pearce.

Digital reprint of the 2017 Bloodaxe Books edition.

for my brother

ACKNOWLEDGEMENTS

Acknowledgements are due to the editors of the following publications where some of these poems first appeared: *Canto, Contourlines* (Salt Publishing, 2009), *Hearing Voices, Interlitq, Jewish Quarterly, Lung Jazz: Young British Poets for Oxfam* (Cinnamon Press, 2012), *Magma, More Raw Material* (The Lucifer Press, 2015), *New Boots and Pantisocracies – the Anthology* (2016), *Poetry Salzburg Review, The Rialto, Stairs and Whispers: D/deaf and Disabled Poets Write Back* (Nine Arches Press, 2017) and *Tryst*. 'Kaddish for Amy' first appeared on the *Eyewear* blog. I should also mention the blog *Peony Moon* and Rebecca Goss's online project *Heart Poems 2014*.

The Oxygen Man was first published as a pamphlet by Five Leaves Press in 2012. I am grateful to Ross Bradshaw, Pippa Hennessy and Cathy Grindrod for taking it on and producing it so beautifully.

I would also like to thank the following readers: Polly Clark, Kaddy Benyon, Lucy Hamilton, Lucy Sheerman, Clare Crossman and Chris Hadley.

CONTENTS

OTHER POEMS

THE OXYGEN MAN

Sister

She will harrow this town, she will turn him up,
whole or in pieces. Being a sister,
she knows that brothers are born to trouble.
Her part is to rescue him,
lend him a heart to face his enemies,
or failing that, confound them herself
with withheld smiles, or with her sharp
big sister's tongue; and if she finds
them gone to ground, their damage done,
she'll cut the losses for both of them
and seek him out, wherever he's lying,
broken and say, *Brother, there's*
no shame in one lost battle, or
in ten. Put the phial down –
don't drink! And if it is too late
for that, she'll scruff the man and stick
her fingers down his throat, or find
an antidote, or make her own,
or heave time back, or failing that,
and even failing that, she'll take him home,
and never mind how small the pieces.

Brother

'Hi,' you said, whenever I picked up: your name
was never asked for. Of course I knew your name.

I can't unknow it now, and you can't make me.
I bagsied it, I chew on it; your name

is ever imminent on my tongue. I start
to talk about my son, but use your name

instead, run two names together just
like Dad would muddle ours – mynameyourname –

as if he had one composite child. Two 'J's,
two final 'n's – we nearly shared a name.

Now I'm Joanne, alone, and call your name.
For pity's sake, pick up.

Chaim

You tipped the liquid curse into your mouth
and knocked it back

    a father lifting his infant daughter
    caught the scent of bitter almonds

    a new PhD in his tasselled cap
    sipped champagne that burned his tongue

    the lager they served in the union bar
    was acrid, and it made him retch

    cycling up the Hill to school
    his hands blurred on the handlebars

    hand over hand, climbing the frame,
    a dizzy head, a failing grip

a baby boy named after life
lost consciousness, then nullified the word.

Welcome to the United States

Halfway to the home of the deceased,
I met a man with the softest voice in all Chicago

and offered him my passport (which,
to give some form to agony, I had almost bitten through).

He took it, and my mother's, apologised so sweetly
for the queue that I forgave him (but not America)

for being what he was. He had brown eyes,
and when he asked the purpose of our visit

and I explained, I thought they brimmed a bit,
like mine were brimming. I felt us

brim together, the soft-voiced man and I;
we were both of us bewildered, and so sorry

and we had to wonder, both of us, why someone
with a family would do a thing like that. *His* brother –

well he was missing for a month, a junkie –
they found him when they dragged the lake –

so I was sorry now for his loss too, we were both
so sorry, and brimming together, and his fingers

were so deft and elegant as they tapped the keys, and how
warm, how tender his feeling heart under his uniform

as shyly, willingly, I ceded him my fingertips,
and offered up my eyes, and believe me, in that moment,

he could have taken everything, that soft-voiced man,
just to give some form to agony, that we might brim together.

From the Best Western

From anywhere to here,
it takes a car.
Up and down the routes, they slice
the country into manageable portions.

Without a car,
it's unintelligible, edgeless:
send your mind to roam on foot,
you'll never get it back.

Minds or persons roam
at their own risk. It's no place
for walkers, with its scarcity
of pavements, its six-lane highways,

its clammy heat, that in the three steps
from the lobby to the car
that's taking you to breakfast,
can hug your breath away.

Your Lawn

Rabbits copy and paste themselves
across a lawn the size of an English churchyard.

Green light shrieks off imported grass,
bred to take the heat once dry,

now saturated from the reservoirs
they built to feed the sprinklers.

It's a lawn for looking at
and mowing. Not for stepping on:

along with shrieking light and rabbits,
it's a home to chiggers,

waiting to hop on board my pasty foreign legs
and burrow in, and itch.

You bought a ride-on mower,
admire your mown and sprinkled lawn

from the safety of the porch.
With all your care, and reservoirs,

the grass has taken well. You did your best
but you weren't bred to take the heat.

Sylar and Elle

Into the midst of things more real
and personal, creep Sylar and Elle.
She is shaking with grief and rage;
he wants to know if he can feel

for someone else, he covets pain.
So he approaches her, this girl
whose father he scalped some episodes back,
and she cries *You!* and zaps him. And again.

I'll kill you! Zap! She hurls blue lightning
from her palms, it hits him dead
in the chest, and he falls back, his arms
spread wide, a T-shaped allusion to something –

make that 'someone' – the viewers know,
and maybe love, and maybe pray to.
Then, in case you hadn't got it,
he gets up. He has no wounds to show

but he looks chastened, and his shirt's
in charcoaled tatters. *I understand,*
he coos. *You hate me. Let me have it:*
I can take it. She slings her hurts

again. Again. The shirt is gone
completely. His body twitches back
to life, as we expect. He's keeping
calm. He's kept his trousers on.

Elle's given up, she's emptied
of her hate. His work complete,
Sylar crawls to her, the blue
sparks in his hands, all mended,

and they laugh. I never want
the scene to end, but it must.
I want to do what Elle does, give it
all to Sylar, but I can't.

Double Act

Straight away they clocked his face on me,
emerging from Arrivals on that unreal night,
crumpled, like a damaged photocopy,

the more disturbing for being almost right.
We had the usual laugh about it, how
they'd known me for his sister at first sight –

an old, familiar joke grown blacker now,
but still compelled to tell itself again
every time I smiled or raised an eyebrow.

All week I was the sick comedienne.
I did my accidental cabaret
for everyone who knew him, mixing pain

with mirth, as satirists always must. I'd play
the part according to the audience:
at breakfast, not quite Daddy; later in the day,

a young professor's echo; always a semblance,
never the real thing, a dreamer's version
of someone lost. I saved my best performance

for his memorial, a grand occasion,
catered, air-conditioned, floral. The crowd
itself, his colleague said, showed the impression

he'd made while he was there. We could be proud:
they hadn't had so many when Craig Venter
spoke. Posthumously, my brother wowed,

and so, accepting the honour as his sister,
I had to say, 'And I thought it was only
a career move for poets.' Laughter,

at this, was slight, and centre stage was lonely.

Night Flight

Nudging slowly into the dawn,
we have no choice. I'm in my seat;
above me in the locker, half
of what is left of you gets thrown

about like Duty Free. Nothing
can be done about this.
I'm sorry, sorry and afraid.
The clammy cabin air is something

I can neither scream nor sleep in.
When I try and watch a movie,
the engine's droning closes over
my ears. We're in a great tin

stomach, and it's digesting us,
noisily, a little every mile.
Here's a distraction at least: the sharp
wail of a toddler in distress,

a couple of rows behind, puke
down his pyjamas. So I think,
'Poor little guy, poor mother.'
I sympathise, I'm feeling sick

myself. The morning light is just
as green, shuffling in like a patient
returning obediently to bed,
where she'll wait quietly for breakfast:

good patients, like good passengers
never press the bell, not even
if they think they might be sick.
They never think to beg their keepers

to let them out, to let them go
right now, because whatever's outside,
dark or empty, it couldn't be worse:
the worst is here. That's all you know.

Notes to an Unwritten Eulogy

1. 'Da-Does': originally supposed to have been a corruption of 'Daddy', but subsequently discovered to mean 'my big sister'.

2. He never weed on her dress on purpose.

3. She only cut his blanket up into tiny pieces because she thought he'd agreed that she should.

4. Sometimes apparently ordinary children turn out to be the offspring of Dr Who, while the old lead-painted cot in their grandparents' box room is actually a Tardis.

5. 'Karate Man': a long-defunct superhero, costumed in a Mothercare dressing-gown.

6. 'Mrs P': although neither party could say what this signified, both understood it to be the worst thing you could possibly call a sister.

7. A 'Marmite face' is the involuntary grimace made when a small quantity of salty yeast extract gets stuck between the upper lip and the gum.

8. By the time he outgrew her, he was already beating her at arm wrestling every time, even when played left-handed.

9. Officially the funniest thing ever is the ping-pong ball that went pk-pk-pk-pk-pk all the way across the top of the radiator and then plonked onto the floor.

10. 'Rekop': a card game invented by the deceased. Similar to poker, except that players must hold their cards in such a way that their hands are visible only to their opponents.

11. 'The Clever One': a controversial title, best left unawarded.

12. The Yiddish proverb that made them laugh so much was: 'Your health comes first: you can always hang yourself later.'

13. Most likely potassium cyanide.

14. The winner is the child who still has a bit of Curly Wurly left when their sibling has none.

Oxygen Man

Today, instead of dying,
you could go to work,
open up the lab
that has your name on it,

power something up –
some expensive toy
it took two grants to buy –
and set creation going.

I said *creation.* I know
the things that you can do:
engineer an enzyme,
speed up evolution;

one of your early tricks
was making oxygen.
Do that once more for me.
Take the manganese ions,

the ones the flowers use,
bind them up with ligands,
stick them in solution,
add your hypochlorite,

wait. We'll wait.
Maybe minutes, hours –
you know, I don't – but then
we'll see the bubbles rise.

Now that's your own good stuff:
breathe it, breathe it in.
Blue is not your colour.
Let everything be green.

Blue-eyed Boy

Dying the way you did,
you reminded me
of how you used to cry,

how the blue would deepen
in your eyes, the apples
ripen in your cheeks,

your mouth release a wail
that couldn't be ignored,
as dismal weather broke

behind your baby lashes,
and when I picture it,
your blue gaze always latches

onto mine, glaring
shock and disappointment,
because I am your sister

and as such I should know,
but clearly don't, exactly
how to stop your tears.

The Door

Every day I stand
in the backwash of your silence,

committing to memory
the idiosyncrasies of your spine

as it curves over a lab bench.
This is your daily struggle

against the problem.
You see nothing else

and you deny me:
I'm only the living

and what can I do?
Only watch.

Only follow you
down the blind corridors,

trying not to lose you
as you flit from door to door,

rattle the handles, thump hard
with the flat of your hand

until you find the one that gives.

Proverbs 6: 5-11

Perhaps you went to the ant
and considered her ways.
You watched;

she provided, she gathered –
meat and food, meat and food –
no guide or overseer,

no ruler, or apparent point.
All those hours
of meatless considering,

they tired you out,
didn't they? I think
you welcomed the hunter,

the fowler too,
I think you welcomed them
and folded your hands.

Not

When I lost my religion,
after a long wasting,
I felt as if I'd been
born again, and when

I say that I mean it was awful
to find myself thrown
naked to the world a second
time, to feel the terrible

rushing in of the real,
but not to have the means
of grabbing hold of it
and bringing it to heel,

and to have no more than snot
and shit and tears to use
to reach whatever's there.
If anything is. Now what?

On Holiday with Cotard

Honestly, the season's over. The sun's
its proper grudging self again,

the trees have given back their borrowed green,
flies are laying final clutches, and soon

they'll rest in spider silk. Rest forever,
rest you well. Now it's time for everyone to relax,

the really thorough way, as you can when everything you fear
the most has happened already

and so you float on loose, float empty
just like the jellyfish, the moons and manes

that blister the sea on the Baltic Coast,
no longer pumping, and therefore not alive.

An Offering

A set of *Trivial Pursuit*, another of possible genes; a pear tree, a tortoise, the ants in the garden; sick and silly jokes, a satellite to bounce them seven hours ahead and back again.

The remote control, the microphone; the meaning and import of certain remarks; the final word, the winning card; the truth about who started what.

Superior height; Bar Mitzvah gifts, a tallis in a tallis bag; a First, a PhD, a lab; a certain way with lucid dreams; a ride-on mower, an early out.

Computer games on audiotape; copies of works by Stanisław Lem; two Emu puppets, two Snoopy dolls; the very last time I made you laugh; whatever you were thinking.

Ageing skin, stiffening joints; a slender orange vase from Gumps; the joke about Dave who knew the Pope; one facetious birthday card; however many years.

The Young Dead Poets

Lovely cop-outs,
they left us behind,
tidying up
in second-best bodies,

straightening backs
and grimacing,
then bending down
to tidy again,

depressing chairs
with leftover bodies,
deleting a line
then writing again,

straining not
to repeat ourselves,
repeating ourselves,
repeating ourselves –

forgive us, please
for repeating ourselves,
for being unlovely
and not copping out,

for staying behind
to tidy up,
to write, to fill
the graceless decades.

THE AUTISTIC ALICE

Alice's Un-Birthday

Alice is three and she knows it.
She's sitting face-to-face with daffodils
underneath the washing-line
which is a roundabout for clothes.

Her mother pegs some clothes up,
gives them all a ride and pegs again.
Alice feels like trying something.
'I'm four,' she says.

'No you're not,' her mother says,
'you're three.' She picks Alice up
and pegs her to this rule:
It isn't saying it that makes it true.

Alice in Check

The bedroom is a battle scene, Alice at one end,
her mother at the other: two queens on a chessboard.

Alice is outnumbered, but she holds her own,
because she fields the Knight Whose Name Is NO!

and boldly he has snicker-snacked his bloody way
straight through her mother's forces. See them on the floor:

the Choking-Collar-Dress, the Orange-Flower-Yucky-Taste,
the Frilly-Dot-Bow-Monster. They want to make Alice

into a girl for looking at, stop her tongue
and force her skin to scream. They should be vanquished,

and would be, if Alice were allowed to win, but not today.
Her mother does the worse thing she could ever do:

Now look – you've made your Mummy cry!
The Knight Whose Name is NO! shakes his wet head

and Alice, who must save them all from being drowned,
gives up, and lets herself be dressed for looking at.

Alice in Reception Class

The paper's waiting on the easel,
brushes in the pots, heads down.
They know how to do it here

and so does Alice: blue strip
makes the sky on top, green strip
lays grass along the bottom.

All the space between is hers.
House in it? Tree? Lady? No:
first line up what's in the pots –

Splodge! goes yellow, orange,
Splodge! the red, the green, and
Splodge! the blue blue blue...

Teacher here: 'That's VERY GOOD!
What IS IT?' 'Splodges,'
Alice says, because they are.

'Oh.' The teacher sounds upset.
She goes. Alice watches colour dance.
Another teacher – different voice,

same words: 'That's VERY GOOD!'
What IS IT?' 'Fireworks?'
tries Alice, to be kind this time.

'LOVELY!' says the teacher.
Alice notes: *The answer they want
isn't what it is – it's what it isn't.*

Big Alice

Without meaning to or even knowing,
Alice has grown huge again.

It starts with her name in an angry voice:
Look what you've done!

Since when were her hands so far away?
One's stuck on her face and covered in ink,

the other's on the desk, by the up-ended carton
with milk seeping out.

Don't just look *at it! Pick it up!*
Alice does, but something's wet somewhere.

'She's got it all over her skirt!'
Alice finds her feet and stands on them,

the scrape of her chair is thunderous and rude.
Go to the office, get a change of clothes.

Eyes watch her thudding damply to the door,
the dumbest Alice-lump they ever saw.

Alice's Walk

If you could feel, as Alice does, how fast the earth is moving

if your bones shuddered at the grinding, forward thrust of it

if you sometimes had to run keep running just to stay in place

if you feared the ground might throw you like a horse its rider

if you knew a foot placed here or there meant life or death

then you wouldn't need to ask her why she walks that way.

In the Garden of Live Flowers

Tiger-lily, Violet, Rose
all bloom where they were planted,
content with themselves, so *pretty*.

Poor Alice, she tries hard
but never really takes.
Tiger-lily, the kindest flower,

says she's a good colour.
'If you could only make your petals
curl a little more...'

Violet, Rose say nothing
to her face, but Alice hears
their rustling asides:

'If I had *petals like Alice's*...'
they snigger. She's a byword
to Violet and Rose,

a joke that runs from bed to bed.
She knows it too. She's not stupid.
'But you look it,' Tiger-Lily says.

'Alice, we're all flowers here,
we're living in a garden
and how we look is everything we are.'

Nothing but a Pack of Cards

Alice is one mile high and she does not care
for stuff and nonsense. She's had enough
of *stupid things* with squeaky pencils,
who take so long to even write their names,
then ask every question but the right one
and only want to write the answers down,
not understand them. Alice understands:
you see more when you're one mile high,
and if you are the only one who understands,
then you *won't* hold your tongue, you *can't* –
they're wrong and they must be told.
'Who cares for *you?*' cries lofty Alice,
'You're nothing but a pack of cards!'
At this they come flying down upon her
and she would try to beat them off,
only she finds herself a normal height,
facing not a pack of cards, but people.
Feeling people. She must beg their pardon.

Alice Between

Between is stone sometimes;
other times, it's vapour.

It freezes her halfway down
a flight of stairs.

It ripples over the bath
where hot water meets cold air;

when she gets in, she feels it
happening through her.

Sometimes, she is petrified;
sometimes, she sublimes.

Alice's Face

It's a piece of clothing she can't figure out,
can't line up or fasten. It's uncomfortable,

she fidgets with it, and without thinking
casts it off, forgets that people can see faces

even when they're empty. Their voices
come from far away, apologising to the face,

asking it what the matter is, what it finds
so funny, what it thinks they've done to it.

They suppose it's Alice they're addressing
but it's just her cast-off face,

no more aware of its own motion
than the anorak a smaller Alice

let fly off a pier, the purple anorak
the wind filled out for long enough

to make someone mistake it for a child
and swim out to her rescue. Alice remembers

how she looked down from the pier
to watch the nice man fetch her anorak.

Advice for Alice

Alice, people are not curiosities for you to stare at.
They see you seeing them. They see you back.

People are not chess pieces, to be moved from square to square.
They will not stay where you have put them.

They are not lessons to be learned, or verse to be recited.
They are not information. You can't have them by heart.

Alice, they're not just figures in your dreams. They have their own
and you might not be in them. There's no symmetry,

no equity, no Caucus Race. You could swim an age in tears,
then run yourself bone dry, and still be left without a prize.

Alice, mind you don't confuse your prepositions:
you should be in love *with*, not *at*.

Tiny Alice

Today she's so
slight, That
she's shrunk
out of sight:
a person might
squash her
and they'd
never know.
Such terrible
dangers turn
friends into
strangers,
so, to
preserve
herself,
Alice must
go. Keen
not to
offend,
Alice says
to her
friend,
'I'm sorry,
I'm tired...'
but nobody
hears.
'My words
are so small,
they can't
catch them
at all,'
sighs
minuscule
Alice
as she
disappears.

Alice's Brother

He sits down on the edge of her college bed, and he says, it's different at home without you. Calmer. The cat's stopped talking, the flowers've shut up too. I know the cards will stay in their pack, chess pieces will wait until I've moved them. I don't have to run to stand still anymore.

You don't know what it's like, having a sister who changes size. When you were small I had to put you in my pocket to keep you safe, and when you were huge, you could fill the whole house. I mean the whole house. It's different without you. There's plenty of room.

Alice's It

It Allows A Portrait in Line-Scan at Fifteen
LES MURRAY

Call her 'Alice' if you like, call her 'she', say she is of such an age,
    still it will be ageless, nameless, wordless. It
is a survival, a living memory of being prey, it fears, it jumps it
    watches.
Predators have big eyes and smiles (*Why, Grandma!*); some of
    them are wheeled and weighing tons.
When she meets these eyes, it freezes and plays dead; she has to
    look away to think again.
It squeaks: in fear, at heavy traffic or in joy, at babies, dogs and
    cats.
It has good creature manners, slowly shuts its eyes at cats, offers
    her hand to dogs and caws at crows.
The near-the-ground it understands instinctively; adult humans, not.
Why aren't all relationships symmetrical?
Uncertainty makes living in her skin intolerable. An answer is
    complete or it is not an answer.
Truth is not a thing that bends. Alice with shaved legs, dyed hair
    and eyebrows plucked is not what Alice looks like. For many
    years, it exercised a veto.
It will never understand that other people have to look at her.
    Sometimes she herself forgets.
It lacks a sense of Alice as continuous, so is compelled to rub or
    pick her skin, or bite her cheeks, or twist her limbs about,
    so as to keep her present to itself.
When agitated, it will flick her fingerpads one two three four against
    her thumbnail.
It is repulsed by too-light touch, by fish, by slugs, by water on its
    face.
It is shattered by loud noise, and crowds shave it to ribbons.
To save them both, it shuts down everything that costs too much:
    the sense of other people, the taming of emotion, intelligible
    speech.
When it is spent, it makes her horizontal.

But catch its glutinous attention, and it will keep her wide eyes
    fixed.
It likes to map associations, it likes a list, it iterates.
It is perseverative.
Despite her, with her, it's persistent.
It persists.

The Mad Hatter's Tea Party

The table is a large one.
There's plenty of room

if you're content to eat alone.
Company always crowds together

at one end, where Mad Hatter
holds his court, in his palace

of turned backs and laughter.
Alice sits down, cup in hand.

No one says 'No room!'.
No one says anything at all.

The Hatter tells a funny tale
about a raven. They all laugh.

The Hare tells a funny tale
about a watch. They laugh again.

The Dormouse tells a funny tale
about a treacle well. They laugh,

then Alice says, *Y'know once, when we were at a safari park my
Dad was standing next to the outdoor dolphin pool, and one of the
dolphins backed up to the edge and smashed its tail down in the water,
so Dad got absolutely soaked – and then, the amazing thing was –
it peered over the side and looked at him and actually laughed!*

Silence. The Hare and Dormouse
look at Alice, then at each other,

then at the Hatter, who smiles
and says, 'Y'know once –

oh fuck, I can't remember,
but it was a *hilarious anecdote*.'

The Hatter's told a funny tale
about an Alice. Now they laugh.

Alice's Laws of Interaction

1. Any given pair or group of persons will remain in a state of mutual indifference until a countervailing action is performed.

2. This action can be either neutral (eye contact), friendly (an upward-inflected salutation, such as 'Hell-*o!*') or hostile ('Oy! You!)...

3. ... and is liable to be met by an equal and like – or opposite – reaction from another member of the pair or group...

4. ... which will then provoke a further reaction, and so on, by which means the conversational momentum passes back and forth...

5. ... until the inevitable moment when that momentum, in accordance with the law of social entropy, has sensibly decreased...

6. ... at which point one or more members will begin to abhor the pair or group and will be forced to change its state by leaving it.

Extra law for Alices:

7. To move a less reactive person, such as Alice, from one state to another, stronger-than-usual force must be applied.

The Alice Case

'The problem with Alice,' the Caterpillar says,
　　'is her rigidity of thought.'

'Yes,' says Humpty Dumpty,
　　'and her lack of empathy.'

'Indeed,' says the Caterpillar,
　　'her mind-blindness.'

'Yes,' says Humpty Dumpty,
　　'her inability to read faces.'

'Indeed', says the Caterpillar,
　　'or tone of voice.'

'And then,' says Humpty Dumpty,
　　'there's the flatness of her affect.'

'Alongside,' says the Caterpillar,
　　'the strangeness of her prosody..'

'...as well as,' says Humpty Dumpty,
　　'her adherence to routine.'

'Not forgetting,' says the Caterpillar,
　　'her repetitive behaviours.'

'Or her failure,' says Humpty Dumpty
　　'to understand a joke.'

'Or her lack,' says the Caterpillar,
　　'of any feel for metaphor.'

'Or her inability,' says Humpty Dumpty,
　　'to hold a proper conversation...'

'Excuse me,' says Alice.
      'May I say something?'

'Of course,' says the Caterpillar –
      'you may say something –'

'Yes,' says Humpty Dumpty,
      'and we'll tell you why it's wrong.'

Alice's Antism

Ground is home to her, it's where
her gaze can come to rest,

take stock of what has never changed:
the rainbows in the gutter,

the points and circles of the pouring rain,
the pavement's long squared shoulder.

And every summer the ants turn up,
shiny black and perfectly themselves,

bringing out the ant-shaped joy
by which she knows she's Alice still.

Alice and the Red Queen

Alice takes her first step late;
before she can take a second,
the Red Queen grabs her hand.

Stand up straight! she says,
and stop that, whatever it is!
Alice, are you listening?

With that, the Red Queen
starts yanking Alice
in and out of rooms.

Say hello! she shrieks.
Say thank you! Say your name!
Don't chew your hair like that!

There are others, keeping pace,
but no one has to yank them.
They can run and speak together.

Smile! coos the Queen,
You won't crack your jaw!
Why are you so serious?

Because it is a serious effort,
this running to keep pace
with all the other ones.

Stop sulking! snaps the Queen.
You need a bra! Some heels!
And sit with your legs together!

Growing up makes running harder
but the Queen is merciless,
dragging Alice far from home.

Have some fun! she orders.
Get a boyfriend! Have a drink!
Dance for me, girl! Dance!

Dancing is worse than running:
every bit as fast, but now
there are steps to remember,

and the Queen's still shouting:
You're drifting, Alice!
Look how far ahead the others are!

Alice glances at the Queen
and sees she's now as tall as her.
'Screw you,' she says, and walks.

Alice's Checklist

The glowing core, the living part, of loves and fears that pull or push her, and with them a curiosity, a collecting eye.

The treasures it collects, for purpose, for comfort, for the pleasure of *arranging* them.

The drive to move, the drive to move, sometimes slightly, sometimes faster, sometimes SUDDENLY.

Speech tides, extremes of high and low.

Basic don't-do-thats, manual brakes; the Social Watcher, who applies them; assembles, for her own use, the Library of Social Situations

– also consulted by: the Social Actor, in charge of Gambits, Responses, Vocal Tone and Appropriate Smiling, who maintains herself the Library of Jokes, Quotes, Anecdotes and Supplemental Scripts, and with it the Archive of Personal Information.

Clothes that do not in any way itch, scratch, hurt, dig in, confine, fasten elaborately, expose unduly, irritate with labels or with fussy trims

– but which, at the same time, must be judged by the Social Watcher to be both acceptable and unremarkable for a person of her gender, age and station, so as to serve as local colour.

Comfortable boots or shoes, that do not make a clicking noise, or have jingling zips; flat enough to run away in.

Handbag, with pockets for eventualities, easy fasteners but none of the shiny, jingly, dangly bits that make her want to scream.

The understanding, clutched safe in her palm, that she is an adult now, who can always turn and walk, who can't be made to.

Queen Alice

She did not expect to be a Queen so soon, or ever,
but somehow, there is a crown upon her head
and Alice must act up to it. The Red Queen

has left instructions: *Keep washed, keep combed.*
Wear what women like you wear. Secure
a partner for the dance. Remember eye contact,

smile when they smile; when they look sad,
look sad. Alice stands up straight, she moves
her face until it feels like someone else's,

then she hits the High Street, smiling,
practising her singing, Queenly voice
on all the shop assistants – with time

it rings less false; with years, she even
fools herself. She finds a King, they claim
their castle, which they decorate and fill

with white goods. She births a little prince,
wheels him to Queenly coffee mornings
where she talks, like other Queens,

of Kings and Princes, High Street clothes,
holidays and in-laws, castle decoration,
the purchasing and breakdown of white goods.

She's done well. People meet a Queenly face
and think it's really hers, and after so long,
she thinks they might be right, and wonders

if she only dreamed that other, awkward one,
but if she did, who's that in the looking-glass?
Whose is that unsmiling, sideways stare?

The Annotated Alice

Special interests? I loved books, mostly
books with other worlds in them.

When I was three, I would ask my mother
to take *The Annotated Alice* down for me

so I could see the pictures. I was drawn by
that other girl with the unsmiling level look.

She had adventures. My mother told me
how she fell for miles but wasn't hurt,

made friends with a vanishing cat, grew
and shrank and grew, but whatever her size,

stayed curious. She said I was curious too.
I asked a lot of questions. One day, I asked

what would happen if I went through
the looking-glass. Would I go, like Alice,

into another world? No, she said:
I'd wake up in hospital, being mended,

and I was so disappointed. I never meant
to stay forever on the nonsense side.

OTHER POEMS

The Bus Riders' Creed

We believe that passengers, like motorists, are people, who need
to move from one place to another;

that if their destination is too far for them to walk, they should
have provided safe, efficient means to get them there;

that these means are more efficient shared, and that sharing, as
every toddler knows, is good;

that therefore it is no imposition to take yourself to a public stop,
and wait with other passengers;

nor is it an infringement of your rights to have to wait for transport
while it pauses at other people's stops;

that everyone who can pay pays the same price for the same dis-
tance, and those who can't pay should be helped to pay;

that those who need help to get on should be helped to get on, and
if other passengers can help them, then they should;

that if someone needs your seat more than you do, then you should
stand;

that it is permissible, if there is room, for you to place your stuff
beside you on another seat, but if that seat is then required
by another passenger, you should pick up your stuff and let
the other person sit, because stuff is neither in nor of itself
important;

that the woman with the walking frame moving ever so ever so
slowly onto the bus and down the aisle deserves your patience,
because you would need it in her place, and one day, probably,
you will;

that all the boys and girls who shout into their phones and at each
other deserve your tolerance, because they are young and
having their turn;

that small, friendly children deserve a smile back;

that small, wailing children deserve compassion, and so do their
parents;

that as long you are on the bus, the other passengers are putting
up with you as well, and you should remember that;

that in one life you will be many different passengers;

that they know nothing worth the knowing, who travel only in cars.

You're Not My Dad, John Inman

Got lots of Dads besides my Dad –
television's full of Dads.
Mr Corbett, he's my Dad,
Michael Bentine, also Dad.
Roy Castle is the Singing Dad
and Brian Cant the Voice of Dad,
Kirk and Spock, two halves of Dad,
Playschool, *Play Away* teem with Dad.
John Inman, though, he's not my Dad –
not everyone I love is Dad.

Hospital Psalm

Glory to the Angels of the Entrances,
      clothéd all in slippers and thin gowns,

their breasts adorned with yellowed dressing
      and their arms with drips,

who were wheeled out to sit,
      or came on foot to lean and cough,

who young or old
      have winter in their cheeks,

who even in the rain light up, draw in,
      mingle breath and smoke

then offer them together, for our sakes,
      to the sky.

Mammogram

August is the month
when a possible future
grinds along my breastbone,
grips me by the softest tissue,
pulls on it just long enough,
just hard enough, to let me know
it could rip it away.

Kaddish for Amy

Let us now magnify and sanctify the name of Him
who made and warned us, according to his Will,

who placed in us our soft or hardened hearts,
then blessed or punished us for what they made us do

who put an evil spirit into Saul, then gave a song to David
so he could drive the spirit out.

Let us bless and extol Him, exalt and praise Him,
who, beyond the reach of any song performable,
commands us still to sing.

The Loft Day

Some words have extra meanings
not understood but *felt*:

they mean like a colour in a painting,
they mean like a note in a song;

they mean like I was meaning it
one Sunday in the early 70s

when strong gales shook the grass
from spearmint to white and back again;

our cousins came to visit
but not for any reason, which puzzled me;

I felt pushed to express it all,
the wind, white grass and puzzlement

that made the Sunday other than itself,
so I said, 'This is a *loft* day,'

and when my mother just went *'What?'*
I realised she wasn't *feeling* it.

Swifts

Shrieking hooks,
they lost their purchase on the sky
but they don't care. They tumble
into view, and out again,
unpinned, unplaceable.

A Run Round All Souls

To be alive is to be embarrassed,
a helpless source of mistakes and smells.
I'm running in lycra, which is a mistake:
I smell.
        I know I do. I note how gracelessly
my flat feet strike the ground,
and how my breath
emerges from my blowsy face in puffs,
while in between my feet and face,
things wobble.
        Meanwhile, beneath the soil
I'm shaking just a little, the dead lie blind,
unhearing and unsmelling, beyond disgust.
Helplessly, the dead are kind.

Pretend to be Celia Johnson

Carefully fix your invisible hat. Remember you are a good sort of woman,
correct fare ready in one gloved hand. Your knees, at rest, are close and
    aligned.
Your handbag sits on your lap like a well-trained dog. It is discreetly
    brown.

Sit straight. Turn your head a precise three-quarters, the perfect angle
for respectable English wistfulness. Sigh at the weather, which is dreary
but at least not frightful. You have that to be grateful for. You have so
    much,

really: the husband, the boy, the house; the bag, the gloves and invisible
    hat.
You are one of the fortunate ones, who shops but never has to serve.
Best to get off here. Best get on. With the list of wants in your head

and the household means in your handbag, you seek and find, select and
    pay,
pick up, and smile, and go. So that's that accomplished. A spot of lunch,
a cup of tea – you simply couldn't take another step without it.

Take your gloves off, place your knees together. Do not, however, remove
your invisible hat, not when you are lunching in a public place.
For drinking tea with respectable English wistfulness, you have to wear
    the hat.

When the tea is finished, sigh at the empty cup. Sigh at the empty
seat across the table. Best be getting home now: put the feet up,
rest the old handbag, remove at last the *blasted* hat – oh golly I – so *sorry*!

Your Words

Did I tell you
I had a dream
about us recently?
We were in a café...

I had a dream
that I had died.
We were in a café.
I was telling you

that I had died.
I felt proud that
I was telling you
what dying was like.

I felt proud that
I had a good story:
what dying was like.
You were riveted!

I had a good story
I could share.
You were riveted.
Like after a birth –

I could share
the information.
Like after a birth,
I wanted to show you

the information
for when it was your time.
Preparation is all.
I wanted to show you

for when it was your time –
though we both know
preparation is all
a lot of crap,

though we both know,
as with birth, it's just
a lot of crap,
what happens to us.

As with birth, it's just
our puny attempt to control
what happens to us.
How the Gods must laugh to see

our puny attempt to control.
I've been thinking a lot,
how the Gods must laugh to see
another fucking scan.

I've been thinking a lot
about us recently…
Another fucking scan –
did I tell you?

The View from Crieff

All the view your eyes can eat
starts with a milky sky,
then half-solidifies
into mountains like mauve dowagers,
content to retire behind
a bank of glowering indigo matrons
who push green hills towards you,
insisting you will have some more, you *will*.

Dem Bones

Here's a live body. Out of custom,
I call it mine. I've laid it out
on a table, or valley bottom,
knees up, feet flat
a hip's width apart.

I'm told to allow
my neck to soften, to lengthen
my spine, unlock an elbow,
unlock the other one,
permit the weight of bone

to work it out with gravity.
I tell the ceiling
I find this hard. In a valley
I can only think of running,
and as I speak, my breathing

shallows, prompting the voice
above me to remark
how wonderful it is
that I should live, when I take
so little air. But still I live. I wake

each morning, as I am caused to,
and when I do, I feel the possibility
of movement in the sinew,
enough to shift my bones today,
though they are very dry.

NOTES

Proverbs 6: 5-11 (26)

The relevant biblical passage is as follows:

> 5 Deliver thyself as a roe from the hand of the hunter, and as a bird from the hand of the fowler.
>
> 6 Go to the ant, thou sluggard; consider her ways, and be wise:
>
> 7 Which having no guide, overseer, or ruler,
>
> 8 Provideth her meat in the summer, and gathereth her food in the harvest.
>
> 9 How long wilt thou sleep, O sluggard? when wilt though arise out of thy sleep?
>
> 10 Yet a little sleep, a little slumber, a little folding of the hands to sleep;
>
> 11 So shall thy poverty come as one that travelleth, and thy want as an armed man.

On Holiday with Cotard (28)

Cotard's syndrome is a rare neuropsychiatric disorder which causes sufferers to hold the delusional belief that they do not exist, are dead, putrefying, or missing some of their internal organs.

Alice's It (44)

This poem was written in appreciative response to Les Murray's poem 'It Allows a Portrait in Line-Scan at Fifteen', which is about his autistic son.